A short guide to Israeli apartheid

Alex Snowdon

COUNTERFIRE

A short guide to Israeli apartheid

First published in Great Britain in 2022 by Counterfire,
Bow House, 157 Bow Road, London E3 2SE.
Cover design and layout: Neil Darby

ISBN 978-1-907899-14-0

A catalogue record for this book is available from
the British Library.

Printed and bound in Great Britain.
www.counterfire.org

Contents

Chapter One: Introduction

Israel was established in 1948 by ethnic cleansing of the Palestinians on a massive scale. Over 700,000 Palestinians were expelled from their homes: forced off their own land, with more than 500 Palestinian villages destroyed. They were removed to make way for a new state that explicitly privileged the rights of one group (Jews) over those of another (the indigenous Palestinian Arabs). This was the Nakba, Arabic for catastrophe.

Israel was created as an ethnocracy, an apartheid state, characterised by a regime of Jewish supremacy. At a time of widespread decolonisation, with India gaining independence in 1947, Israel was a new settler-colonial state. Zionism was a movement, emerging in the late nineteenth century, that focused on Jewish settlement in historic Palestine, with a view to it becoming a national home for Jews. It was, according to the Zionists, a land without a people for a people without a land.

Zionism was a response to widespread antisemitism in Europe. Antisemitism reached its horrifying climax in the Holocaust, which galvanised international sympathy for the Zionist project. However, Palestine was not a land without a people. Rather than being the desert of Zionist imagination, it was a cosmopolitan society with a substantial Palestinian population.

Zionist terror gangs killed Palestinians and forced huge numbers out of their homes during 1947-9. The result was a state that treated those Palestinians who remained inside Israel's borders as second-class citizens. Palestinians outside Israel became the world's largest refugee community. In 1967, Israel further expanded its territory, bringing large numbers of Palestinians under its military rule. The logic of expansion is built into the very foundation of Israel as a settler-colonial state, seeking land at the expense of the indigenous population.

Israel has always required Western imperialist backing. In 1917, Zionist ambitions were boosted by the Balfour Declaration, which pledged Britain's support for the aspiration to a Jewish national home. Jewish settlement in Palestine grew under the British Mandate after World War One. Once Israel was established, it was the US that became the primary imperial sponsor, especially from the 1960s onwards. The US increasingly saw Israel as a crucial strategic ally in the Middle East.

The Oslo 'peace process' of the 1990s did nothing to redress the historic injustices faced by the Palestinians. It entrenched the idea that Palestinians could only aspire to a separate state occupying a fraction of historic Palestine, while Israel greatly expanded its settlements in the occupied West Bank. It had nothing to offer the Palestinians suffering inequality and discrimination inside Israel or those living in east Jerusalem. It was silent on the Palestinian refugees (or their right of return) exiled outside of Palestine altogether.

Today's reality is a system of apartheid. There is, in truth, a single apartheid state stretching from the Mediterranean Sea to the Jordan River. Israel controls all this territory and subjects Palestinians to oppression that varies in form. Israel systematically treats the Palestinians as an unwanted presence and a demographic threat, so racism is inevitably a core part of its ideology.

Nearly two million Palestinians live as second-class citizens inside Israel. A further five million Palestinians live in the West Bank or Gaza, the territories occupied by Israel since 1967, or in east Jerusalem (which was annexed in the same year). An estimated six million more Palestinians live as refugees outside historic Palestine, many of them in neighbouring countries like Jordan, Lebanon and Syria, denied the right of return to their homeland.

The West Bank is under Israeli military occupation with

over 500 checkpoints, hundreds of miles of separation wall, and thousands of Israeli Defence Force soldiers protecting the settlements in which ever-increasing numbers of Jewish Israelis reside. The settlements are deemed illegal by the International Court of Justice. Gaza is under siege by land, air and sea, strangled by Israel's crippling economic blockade and repeatedly subjected to deadly military assaults. East Jerusalem is squeezed by Israel's determination to move its own Jewish citizens in and the Palestinians out.

There is huge economic inequality between Israelis and Palestinians. Acute poverty is widespread in the Occupied Territories; the Palestinian economy as a whole is prevented from developing, as part of a broader process of exploitation and subjugation.

Israel is famously a recipient of a vast amount of US 'overseas aid' (£2.7 billion in 2020 alone), while international aid of a different kind is essential for many desperately poor Palestinians. Israeli policy towards Gaza has been to keep it permanently on the edge of a humanitarian catastrophe, as a deliberate policy intended to suppress resistance and self-organisation.

It is the Palestinians inside Israel who have been most overlooked in discussions about Palestine, especially since the Oslo process firmly reduced the officially-approved horizons for Palestinian advance to the occupied territories alone. They have often been perceived as passive and quiescent; it has even been suggested that they have been successfully incorporated into Israeli politics, and neutered as a source of opposition through a process of 'Israelisation'. Passivity has never been the whole picture, however, and it was certainly never true that Palestinians in Israel had become entirely cut off from the Palestinian struggle.

In a 2021 *Guardian* article, Nimer Sultany (now based in London) wrote of his own experiences as a Palestinian inside Israel. He recalled being educated in separate

Arab schools (from kindergarten to high school), being blocked from renting a flat while at university due to his Palestinian background, needing medical attention after an assault by Israeli police officers when he was a young lawyer, and the routine nature of being racially profiled at the airport whenever he travelled abroad. All of these experiences are testament to the systemic nature of inequality, discrimination and racism in Israel.

Sultany wrote that 'coexistence is a fiction that conceals a reality of separate and unequal lives'.[1] In hundreds of Jewish Israeli communities, there are neighbourhood committees that can – and do – legitimately deny Palestinians permission to move there. The notion of Israel as a Jewish state is enshrined in Israeli law and in the constitution. Israeli courts routinely sanction the transfer of Palestinian land to Jews. Nearly half of Palestinians live below the poverty line, while unemployment for the Palestinian minority is around 25%.

Diana Buttu, Palestinian lawyer and citizen of Israel, refers to 'coexistence' by Palestinians and Jewish Israelis as a myth. She writes: 'We Palestinians living in Israel "sub-exist," living under a system of discrimination and racism with laws that enshrine our second-class status and with policies that ensure we are never equals.' Palestinians are 20% of Israel's population of around nine million, yet over sixty discriminatory laws have been enacted to enforce Palestinians' second-class status.[2]

This little book is, among other things, about changing the narrative on Israel and Palestine. It is the story of an apartheid state: how it was constructed, what it means for those who suffer under it, and how it is sustained to this day. It is not, as politicians and media would have us believe, a two-sided conflict between different camps that requires a 'peace process' to resolve the conflict, and separate states for the two sides. It is a story of colonisation, of dispossession through violence, that starts before Israel's foundation in 1948 and continues to this day.

To make sense of today's grim reality, we must return to the Nakba and to the processes of colonialism, nationalism and Zionism that fed into the expulsion of the Palestinians from their land. This historical perspective is the focus of the next four chapters. I will move on to examine the injustices facing Palestinians today, Palestinian responses to those injustices, and the role of international solidarity movements in later chapters.

Understanding the truth about Palestine provides the basis for charting a way forward. When we frame the issues correctly, we can start to see how things might be done differently. The case for what is often called a 'one-state solution', a secular and equal state across historic Palestine, arises from this analysis.

Ultimately, a single democratic state, which would respect the rights of Palestinians and Jews alike, is required across the whole of Palestine. Only such an alternative can fulfil the rights, aspirations and needs of all the Palestinian people.

Chapter Two: Imperialism

Arthur James Balfour signed a short letter on 2 November 1917. Though brief, it would have historic ramifications. Balfour was Tory foreign secretary in a Liberal-led wartime coalition. The short note he signed pledged British support for the project of Zionist colonisation in historic Palestine. It would come to be known as the Balfour Declaration. It stated:

> 'His Majesty's Government view with favour the establishment in Palestine of a national home for the Jewish people, and will use their best endeavours to facilitate the achievement of this object, it being clearly understood that nothing shall be done which may prejudice the civil and religious rights of existing non-Jewish communities in Palestine, or the rights and political status enjoyed by Jews in any other country.'

Three decades later, this 'national home for the Jewish people' would be established through the forced dispossession of the Palestinians who already lived there. Such a state could, as Balfour knew, only be founded on the back of violent displacement.

Balfour's declaration was addressed to the wealthy aristocrat, Walter Rothschild and expressed support for the British Zionist Federation. It gave official approval to the idea of a 'homeland' that would explicitly privilege one particular group, Jews, at that time scattered across the world, over the indigenous inhabitants of the territory. The drive to colonise, to steal land by violent means, and subjugate or expel the people it is stolen from, would consequently be built into the Israeli state at its foundations. The Balfour Declaration was the prelude to that.

Balfour and his colleagues were no friends of the

Jewish people, who were victims of racist discrimination and demonisation throughout much of Europe (Britain included). In 1905 Balfour had, as Prime Minister, been responsible for legislation that sought to stop Jews fleeing persecution in Russia from coming to Britain.

Opposition to the declaration within the British Cabinet came from Sir Edwin Montagu, Secretary of State for India and the only Jewish Cabinet member, who declared that the majority of British Jews were opposed to Zionism. He was right: it was then a minority current. His main concern was that a separate Jewish homeland gave legitimacy to the then widespread antisemitic notion that Jews were not welcome in Europe.

In 1917, the dominant figures in the British political establishment viewed Zionist aspirations sympathetically because they fitted British imperial concerns. One of these concerns was a desire to control the Suez Canal, which was vital for trade. Another was the maintenance of communications with India and their east African colonies. There was also a desire to secure a strong base in the Middle East for access to oil. Economic self-interest underpinned British sponsorship of Jewish settlement in Palestine.

Balfour's declaration betrayed contempt for the indigenous Palestinians, who then formed 86% of Palestine's population. The Declaration was notable for pledging that they would have 'civil and religious rights', but with no mention of political rights. The implication was clearly that Palestinians would be subordinated to Jewish settlers in their own land. In reality, of course, the establishment of a Jewish state would only be possible via ethnic cleansing and mass dispossession.

After the end of World War One, the Middle East was carved up by the victors. The partitioning of the defeated Ottoman Empire brought new territory under the control of Britain and France. The Sykes-Picot agreement of 1916 (between Britain and France) and the Balfour Declaration contributed to this colonial enterprise. Palestine, from the

Mediterranean Sea in the west across to the Jordan River in the east, had previously been under Ottoman rule. It became a British Mandate territory under the auspices of the League of Nations (a body dominated by Britain and France) after World War One.

During the years of the British Mandate, British authorities oversaw increased Jewish settlement while brutally suppressing Palestinian resistance, especially during the period of mass revolt and strike waves between 1936 and 1939. This laid the ground for the establishment of Israel through the Nakba, when Zionist terror drove Palestinians from their land.

The notion of 'a land without a people', of Palestine as a largely barren desert, is integral to the founding mythology of Israel and has persisted ever since. Ilan Pappe, the Israeli historian, counteracts this mythology when he writes: 'Palestinians spoke their own dialect, had their own customs and rituals, and appeared on the maps of the world as living in a country called Palestine.'[3]

Nur Masalha, the Palestinian historian, has written of 'the four thousand year history' of Palestine. Palestine was certainly a geographically distinct entity from Roman times onwards. It was a province of the Roman Empire and continued to be regarded as a fairly cohesive geopolitical space during the centuries that followed. It was a province of the Ottoman Empire from 1517 onwards. This is important to acknowledge because pro-Israel revisionists sometimes suggest that Palestine was never really a place to begin with, just as they suggest that the Palestinians were never a national or ethnic group.

Palestine became a thriving and cosmopolitan society, mostly rural but with significant urban settlements and some economic development. It had many coastal towns, with ports (like Haifa and Jaffa) that were crucial for trade with Europe, and further inland a lot of rich agricultural land. Ottoman records of 1878 indicate a population of 462,465 people. The vast majority were Muslim, around 10% were Palestinian

Christians, and a little over 3% were Jewish. These were Jews rooted in Palestinian life and culture over generations, before the wave of settlement that followed.

The prevalent late-nineteenth-century ideas of nationalism affected Palestine and other parts of the eastern Mediterranean. The Palestinian elite developed a stronger sense of self-determination and demanded greater autonomy within the Ottoman Empire. Across the Arab world, especially in the urban centres and among the middle classes, the interconnected notions of nationhood and self-government gathered steam.

The sense of a national identity, defined by such things as shared territory, culture and language, became stronger in this period. This was a secular identity, not one defined by religion or sect. And the idea of achieving more political autonomy, or even complete independence, on the basis of nationhood was connected with this.

After the collapse of the Ottoman Empire, Palestinians' self-image as a distinct national group deserving its own independent state was strengthened. This was in some tension, though, with both the reality of British colonial oversight and the increasing settlement of the land by Jews. Zionist settlement began, initially on a small scale, in 1882. There is a story from the early days of settlement of two rabbis looking out at the land. One observes its beauty. The other agrees, but adds a cautionary note: 'the bride is beautiful but married to another man.'

This underpins why the pre-1948 Zionist project, and subsequently the state of Israel, are best understood as examples of settler colonialism. There are historical examples of settler colonialism to be found in Canada, the US, Australia, New Zealand and South Africa, where white European settlers were confronted by the reality of indigenous people already living in the territory they wished to colonise. These are histories of colonialism, violence and racism. It was never likely to be very different in Palestine if the settlers insisted on making grand claims to the land to which they moved.

Chapter Three: Zionism

Zionism is a political movement which grew out of three interlinked phenomena. It was a response to antisemitism, it was one expression of the much wider phenomenon of nationalism, and it was sponsored by Western imperialism. The Zionist movement and its ideology need to be understood as a particular version of the nationalism that was prevalent in the late nineteenth and early twentieth centuries: a settler-colonial nationalism that depended upon a close relationship with imperialism.

The roots of its nationalism were not in a particular territory, but in shared Jewishness. The dominant political trend in the Zionist movement aspired to create a Jewish homeland in historic Palestine. It demanded 'a land without people for a people without a land.'

The Zionist movement emerged, from the 1880s onwards, in response to European racism. Antisemitism was a long-established form of racist prejudice and discrimination in Europe and Russia. The French Revolution had represented a leap forward for European Jewry. Newer and more rational ideas, together with democratic aspirations, challenged the old ideologies, of which antisemitism was very much a part. Nonetheless, antisemitism persisted, and was in some ways refashioned, as capitalism developed.

Pseudoscientific justifications for racism were developed. This could be seen in attempts to justify the biological racism, which characterised black people as inferior and backward, that became more pronounced as European capitalism gobbled up more and more land and resources in the 'Scramble for Africa' from around 1870 onwards. It was also expressed in the caricaturing of Jews within Europe as embodying alien practices and posing a threat to modern capitalism.

Antisemitism in its modern form was therefore an ideology in the service of capitalism and imperialism, not merely a hangover from medieval Europe. The Nazis held the view that Jews were both biologically inferior and a destabilizing 'enemy within'. Wealthier Jews were caricatured as parasites, while working-class Jews were strongly associated with left-wing ideas, in particular the hated Bolshevism. These prejudices were part of the European political mainstream, but were taken to their murderous extreme by Nazi Germany in the Holocaust.

The Zionist movement was only ever one political current among Jews, and for a long time it attracted only a very small minority. The First Zionist Congress, which launched the Zionist Organisation, took place in 1897. For many years afterwards, the Zionists, led by Theodor Herzl, struggled to muster much support. There were many anti-Zionist Jews (often socialists) and non-Zionist Jews.

The dominant views in Jewish communities involved seeing antisemitism as something that had to be challenged and overcome within the societies in which Jews lived. Zionism, by contrast, reflected a degree of fatalism on that score, resigned as it was to seeking a 'homeland' elsewhere.

Zionism did not begin with a clear commitment to having a homeland in Palestine. Different options were considered. During the early twentieth century, however, Zionist aspirations crystallized around the notion of making a home in Palestine. This drew on old scriptural references to the region in the Jewish religion for ideological support. In 1901, when only 4% of the population of Palestine was Jewish, the Jewish National Fund was established. Its aim was to acquire land in Palestine for Jewish settlement.

The Zionist project took a more concrete and coherent form during the years immediately prior to, and following, the Balfour Declaration in three different ways. As already mentioned, it became very sharply focused on Palestine.

Secondly, it evolved from the vague notion of a 'homeland', which could theoretically involve living side by side with other national or ethnic groups as part of a larger nation state, towards the distinct idea of a Jewish nation state.

Thirdly, it became clear that Britain would be the effective colonial sponsor. Zionism could never stand a chance without the active support of at least one imperialist state, because it involved making claims to territory that was already inhabited. In 1896, Herzl had written that a Jewish state in Palestine would 'form a part of a wall of defence for Europe in Asia, an outpost of civilisation against barbarism.'[4] Racist contempt for Arabs flowed inevitably from this colonial perspective. Chaim Weizmann, Israel's first president, once said: 'There is a fundamental difference in quality between Jew and native.'[5]

This vision of a nation state was fuelled by both the wider trend of nationalism and by European racism towards non-European people. Imperialist assumptions underpinned the idea that it would be perfectly reasonable to take over the land of people in the Middle East. It was always debatable whether Jews were really 'a people without a land', as it could be argued that Jews ought to stay in the countries where they were settled: whether rooted in the left-wing vision of anti-racist working-class unity with non-Jews, or a moderate commitment to assimilation into European society. Nevertheless, the notion of 'a land without a people' was undoubtedly false: Palestine was already peopled, inconveniently for the Zionists, by Palestinians.

Jewish settlement grew gradually from the start of the twentieth century onwards, encouraged by a desire to escape the racism and poverty that afflicted many European Jews, and the more violent and overt antisemitic pogroms in Russia. After the Balfour Declaration, once the British Mandate was established, the numbers grew substantially. In the 1920s and 1930s there was growing antagonism, including on occasions deadly violence, between Jewish incomers and the indigenous population.

Having referred to Zionism as a form of settler colonialism in the previous chapter, it is necessary here to clarify and develop what is meant by that. Classic colonialism involved strong European states taking over and colonizing lands elsewhere in the world and politically subjugating the people. These colonies were formally part of an empire, run by one of Europe's great powers, and there was no self-rule or democracy. This was the global order that developed between 1870 and 1914.

These empires were characterized by sharp economic exploitation and also by the promotion of racist attitudes towards the 'colonials' among the population of the imperialist state. An elite layer within the colonized population might be incorporated, politically and economically, into the empire, but only to an extent. Senior administration would still rest with foreign officials from the imperialist state, while prospects for economic development would be retarded.

Settler colonialism is distinct from this in a number of ways. Settler colonies are run by people who have a degree of independence from the European imperialist power that originally settled some of its people there. In the American case, this went as far as the settled domestic elites launching a successful war of independence against Britain. So the settler population, while broadly sharing the ideological attitudes of white Europeans towards the 'natives', sought independence (to greater or lesser degrees) from their initial European colonial sponsor.

Settler colonialism has also been motivated, to a very large degree, by the wish to possess land. It has tended to be expansionist, seeking more and more land, irrespective of who already lives there. This, in turn, meant conflict with indigenous populations. The expansion into the 'Wild West' by the American pioneers of the nineteenth century is the archetypal example.

Genocide has therefore been a greater feature of settler colonialism than classic colonialism. The people are in the way of control of the land, so the people must be removed. That can happen either through exiling them or killing them. Very often it has been the latter.

This appalling logic of settler colonialism can be seen all too graphically in Zionism's development and, as we will see in the next chapter, the foundation of Israel as a 'Jewish state'. Kibbutzim, collective farms and plots of land, started in the 1920s or 1930s, could often seem egalitarian (and even socialist) because of their cooperative ideals and internal equality. However, they excluded the Palestinians, with Palestinian farmers removed from land that settlers had bought from absent landowners. The settlers living there tended to have a deeply hostile stance towards the Palestinians, who were viewed as a nuisance or a threat.

As Jewish immigrants became more settled in Palestine, during the 1920s and 1930s, they tended to develop a highly confrontational relationship with the Palestinians, rooted in conflict over control of land. A sense of superiority to the indigenous Palestinians was part of the expansionist settler mentality. Conflict arose precisely because Europeans were seeking to settle in a land that didn't belong to them and was already populated. The lived reality of settler colonialism was the breeding ground for racist attitudes towards the indigenous Palestinians. This continues to be true today.

Israeli apartheid and violence have their roots in this pre-history of the Israeli state. Apartheid policies are no aberration, but rooted in the very foundation stones of Israel as a racially exclusive settler-colonial state.

Chapter Four: Catastrophe

Momentum towards the establishment of Israel accelerated under the impact of Nazi Germany's persecution of the Jews from 1933 onwards, generating huge numbers of Jewish refugees. European states, including the UK, were reluctant to accept the refugees, even during World War Two. The Holocaust, involving the murder of at least six million Jews in the death camps of Nazi-occupied Europe, saw a third of the world's entire Jewish population eradicated. It was the most extreme manifestation of European imperialism and of the racism that accompanied it.

When a shocked world learnt of the extermination camps and gas chambers, it generated widespread sympathy for Jews and for their aspirations. Within the Jewish community there was growing support for the Zionist project, though still very unevenly. The Holocaust massively strengthened the idea that Jews were not welcome in Europe and needed to create a home elsewhere. It boosted the notion of separation from European society. Jews – expelled by the Nazis and spurned by the countries in which they sought refuge – had little alternative.

This wasn't the only significant background to the establishment of Israel though. Two other things mattered enormously. One was the growth in the numbers of Jews living in Palestine that had already taken place prior to 1939. These 'facts on the ground' laid the basis for further expansion.

The other important historical trend was at the global level. The geopolitical map was being redrawn after the defeat of Nazi Germany and its allies by the allied powers. As the Cold War got underway, spheres of influence were established for the US and its allies and, on the other hand, the Soviet Union.

Decolonization gathered pace. India, the jewel in the crown of the British Empire, gained its independence (and underwent partition between India and Pakistan) at the same time as the establishment of Israel. Huge parts of Africa and Asia saw the establishment of independent countries, still to a large extent shaped economically by the global imperialist system, but nonetheless formally independent. Israel's establishment was part of the post-war remaking of the world, while also being highly anomalous: a settler-colonial state established at a time of rapidly accelerating decolonization.

Israeli propaganda has subsequently presented the Palestinian Nakba as a case of Palestinians voluntarily leaving their land in 1948. While 15 May is marked by Palestinians as Nakba Day each year, it is celebrated as Independence Day by Israel. This is a curious perversion of language, stealing the vocabulary of decolonization and national liberation to symbolize the birth of a settler-colonial state that dispossessed those whose families had lived there for generations.

In the 1930s, the Zionists already knew that establishing a 'homeland' of the type they desired would inevitably require the removal, or 'transfer', of the Palestinians who lived in the territory over which they craved control. David Ben-Gurion (who would later become Israel's first prime minister) told a Zionist conference in 1937: 'In many parts of the country new settlement will not be possible without transferring the Arab fellahin.'[6] Elsewhere he wrote: 'With compulsory transfer we would have a vast area for settlement … I support compulsory transfer.'[7] At this time, the Zionists tended to imagine the British overseeing such transfers of Palestinians, indicating the close and dependent relationship that Zionist settlers had with British colonialism.

The publicly-declared Zionist position of support for 'voluntary transfer' of some Palestinians masked an awareness, at least among the movement's leaders, of the need for compulsory removal of significant numbers from their homes and land. That would require force. It simply wasn't logical or plausible to advocate a Jewish state that would somehow not involve the forcible, where necessary violent, removal of large numbers of Palestinians.

Jewish settlement in Palestine continued during and after World War Two. This forms an important part of the background to the founding of Israel. The widespread horror at the Holocaust forms the backdrop to increased international sympathy for the idea of a Jewish state. But it was the British announcement of withdrawal from Palestine in February 1947 – reflecting the limits of British imperial power after 1945 - that can be considered the catalyst for the events that led to the Nakba. The day of 15 May 1948 would be set as the date for the British Mandate to end.

In November 1947, the recently-formed United Nations published its Partition Plan. The UN had taken responsibility for negotiating and planning the future of Palestine in the light of the British withdrawal announcement. The plan was heavily skewed towards the Jewish population. Palestinian Arabs formed over two thirds of the population, yet the plan was to grant 55.5% of all Palestinian territory to the Jewish minority. Even inside the proposed new Jewish state, Palestinians would make up nearly half of the population.

Palestinians were being told, without any consultation, that a settler minority would be taking over control of more than half of historic Palestine. This could not reasonably be regarded a just settlement. Yet the Zionist movement, inside Palestine and internationally, launched a propaganda drive characterizing it is as unduly generous to the Palestinians. They engaged in serious lobbying. And they prepared for using force to get what they wanted.

The Nakba was, in the words of Karma Nabulsi, 'driven by a single strategic aim: to rid the land of the native inhabitants of Palestine in order to establish a new

state for European settlers in their place.'[8] In practical
terms this meant, as Nabulsi puts it, 'military raids and
sieges, bombardments and forced convoys, and the many
massacres over the spring and summer of 1948.' The total
destruction of more than 500 Palestinian villages was
geared towards expelling Palestinians, but also making it
harder for them to return. The architects of the new Israeli
state were determined to erase Palestine from the map:
to destroy the concept of Palestine as a geographical or
political entity.

An estimated seventy massacres took place. The
most notorious was the village of Deir Yassin, where the
Irgun (the Zionist terror gang) boasted of killing all 110
inhabitants of the village. Some were killed in their beds;
others were lined up and shot. Menachem Begin, a future
Israeli prime minister, was head of the Irgun and took
pride in the massacre. The Deir Yassin massacre inspired
terror in other Palestinian villages and encouraged many
Palestinians to flee.

The result of Zionist terror was 13,000 Palestinians
killed and more than 700,000 expelled. The new Israeli
state occupied 78% of the land of historic Palestine, far
more than envisaged in the UN partition plan. In 1949, the
UN famously adopted Resolution 194, endorsing the right
of return for Palestinians. It stated:

'The refugees wishing to return to their homes and live
at peace with their neighbours should be permitted to
do so at the earliest possible date … Compensation
should be paid for the property of those choosing not
to return.'

Despite this call being reaffirmed a great many times
by UN bodies since 1949, Israel has always disregarded
it. Israel created a web of laws preventing Palestinians
from returning home and reclaiming land, seeking to
legitimise the new state's confiscation of homes and lands.
Palestinians retained the keys to their old homes (the key

subsequently became the symbol of Palestinian refugees'
struggle) and the demand for the right of return would be
at the core of Palestinian political aspirations in the 1950s
and 1960s. Israel, meanwhile, has tried to make the Nakba
invisible: to erase it from history, as that assists its project
of erasing Palestine and the Palestinians.

Chapter Five: Occupation

If 1948 is the most important year in the history of Palestine and Israel, 1967 is the second most important. It became a major turning point as it marked the start of an occupation of even more Palestinian territory that continues today. The West Bank and the small (but densely-populated) Gaza Strip became occupied territory, while east Jerusalem (including the historic Old City) was annexed by Israel. Gaza was taken from Egypt and the West Bank from Jordan.

Israel's victory over the Arab states in the Six-Day War of June 1967 led to the occupation. The word 'occupation' is misleading though; the word conventionally refers to a temporary state of affairs, yet this is now over a half-century old and seemingly irreversible. Israel has never abided by the Geneva Conventions governing the conditions of occupation, which expressly prohibit occupiers seizing land and settling parts of their population on it.

The events of 1967 can only be understood in the context of 1948. Israeli political and military leaders regarded the Nakba as unfinished business. The Zionist movement had struck a deal with Jordan's leaders in 1948: it would restrain itself from trying to seize the whole of historic Palestine, from the Mediterranean Sea across to the Jordan River in the east (bordering Jordan), in exchange for Jordan showing military restraint in 1948. However, Israeli leaders were subsequently frustrated by this compromise. Ben-Gurion called it a 'fatal historical mistake' to have allowed Jordan control of the West Bank after 1948.

Israeli elites had been planning how Israel might seize this territory for years before they had the opportunity in June 1967. The Israeli rationale for occupying the

West Bank doesn't hold up. It is that Israel was merely responding to Jordanian provocation. If that was true, it doesn't even begin to explain why it has maintained the occupation for decades beyond when the military conflict of that year was resolved.

Since 1967, the Israeli state has formally paid lip service to a 'two-state solution', the notion of an independent Palestinian state existing alongside Israel. The facts on the ground have always pointed in a different direction: towards permanent occupation, expansion of Jewish Israeli settlement, and the erasure of any prospect of a Palestinian state. The settlements have encroached on (and fragmented) Palestinian territory, while being used to justify a massive and draconian military infrastructure, policing the everyday lives of Palestinians.

After 1967, a complex picture developed. Palestinians inside Israel were no longer formally under military law, as had been the case up to 1966, but they suffered systematically from discrimination, inequality and racism. Both Gaza and the West Bank were under a military occupation that was ostensibly temporary, yet remains in place over half a century later (around 300,000 Palestinians fled these occupied territories in the wake of the 1967 war, many of them becoming refugees for a second time). Israel began building settlements in these occupied territories in the 1970s, accompanied by increasingly repressive measures towards Palestinians by the military. Annexed East Jerusalem (historically Arab) was also a site for Jewish settlement and for state harassment of Palestinians.

Israel also, during this period, became an indispensable ally of the US: a watchdog for US imperialism in the Middle East. It became the recipient of growing amounts of US overseas aid, largely in the form of military spending and support. Israel's 1967 victory was followed by another military victory over neighbouring Arab states in 1973. In subsequent years there would be moves towards the Arab states normalising relations with Israel, notably in the Egypt-Israel peace treaty signed in 1979, However, this would be a major source of tension between the Arab elites and the Arab streets, with many ordinary Arabs angry with their leaders' betrayals of the Palestinian cause.

The Iranian Revolution of 1979 meant the loss of a vital US ally in the Middle East, giving Israel even greater importance than before. Israel's invasion of Lebanon in 1982, and occupation of some Lebanese territory in the following years, indicated its highly aggressive nature, and wider role in the region. Israel and the US have been closely allied in opposition to Iran and any perceived proxies for Iran, for example Hezbollah in Lebanon, since this period.

There was always resistance from Palestinians to Israel's treatment of them inside Israel, in the occupied territories and beyond. The Palestine Liberation Organisation, founded in 1964, gave expression to Palestinian aspirations for self-determination. The PLO was politically dominated by Fatah, a Palestinian party founded by Yasser Arafat and others in 1959. It was widely seen as embodying and directing a struggle for national liberation, including through armed struggle. It had a deep commitment to the right of return for Palestinian refugees and rejected the Israeli state altogether, embracing support for what has often been dubbed a one-state solution, i.e. a single secular state encompassing the whole of historic Palestine.

However, the PLO changed considerably over time. Ilan Pappe writes:

'Fatah is a secular national movement, with strong left-wing elements, inspired by the Third World liberation ideologies of the 1950s and 1960s and in essence still committed to the creation in Palestine of a democratic and secular state for all. Strategically, however, Fatah has been committed to the two-states solution since the 1970s.'[9]

This profound strategic reorientation emerged from failure and frustration. The brutal reality of military occupation became more entrenched, settlement building expanded, territory became more fragmented, and Israel appeared unstoppable. The US backed Israel, while Arab governments made their peace with Israel, and, after the Cold War ended, a geopolitical order shaped by US power seemed more powerful than ever. This provides the backdrop to the PLO's disastrous shift towards a fruitless set of negotiations in the 1990s, which expressed an acute narrowing of aspirations to a merely impoverished Palestinian 'state' on West Bank territory.

The 1980s saw a change for the worse in Palestinians' living standards. Falling oil prices led to falling demand for Palestinian migrant workers in the Gulf states. A collapse in the Israeli stock market led to problems for Palestinian workers in Israel: a fall in income combined with the tightening of work opportunities for Palestinians, accompanied by discrimination and abuse.

The growth of Jewish settlements inside the Occupied Territories involved the theft of Palestinian land, damaging the local economy. Israeli policy became more belligerent, shifting away from seeking consent and accommodation. All these factors influenced the emergence of the first intifada, the militant rebellion by Palestinians against oppression, which started in December 1987.

The Oslo 'peace process' in the 1990s did nothing for the Palestinian economy; indeed there was a fall in living standards, which was (again) one factor behind the eruption of resistance in the start of the second intifada in 2000. A major problem in these years was the increasing curtailment of employment opportunities for Palestinians seeking work inside Israel. Growing poverty and discrimination fed bitterness and disillusionment. Edward Said described the Oslo Accords as 'an instrument of Palestinian surrender, a Palestinian Versailles.'

A gulf opened up during the Oslo years (1993-2000): while the Israeli economy boomed, the Palestinian economy contracted. For Palestinians, poverty and unemployment grew. Living standards fell still further after 2000, when Palestinians in Gaza and the West Bank became increasingly reliant on overseas aid to avoid humanitarian disaster. In the West Bank, the Palestinian Authority (PA) has failed to improve conditions even marginally for the local population.

The Palestinian Authority was formed to administer the Occupied Territories partially, but within a framework of a brutally repressive and unjust military occupation, and a deliberately weakened economy. This has meant that the PA has been deeply compromised since it was founded. The Oslo process also strengthened the view that the situation in historic Palestine was a two-sided violent conflict between Israelis and Palestinians. There were, according to this account, competing groups with competing claims. Fundamentally, it was a conflict between two sides.

This conflict was, as time wore on, more and more narrowed to being focused on the Occupied Palestinian Territories. The idea of a separate Palestinian state in this territory (or at least large parts of it) dominated the so-called peace talks. This 'two-state solution' took for granted the continuing existence of a second-class Palestinian population inside Israel. It equally took for granted the prohibition of millions of displaced Palestinian refugees from returning to their homeland.

Oslo therefore expressed a profound narrowing of aspirations on behalf of the Palestine Liberation Organisation. The outcome was hopeless for the Palestinians. The extremely limited autonomy for the PA cemented an elite layer among the Palestinians into helping manage the occupation, however uneasily.

Chapter Six: Apartheid

Having outlined the history of Israeli apartheid and the oppression of the Palestinians, from the Balfour Declaration and the emergence of Zionism through to the failures of Oslo, we now turn to present-day conditions. The next chapter will examine the incorporation of a Palestinian political and administrative elite – the privileged upper echelons of a professional middle class - into a complicit role in Israeli settler colonialism. Subsequent chapters will examine the international context, including the rise of solidarity movements and the backlash against them, and the emergence of a new wave of Palestinian resistance, concluding with a look at the current prospects for justice.

There has always been Palestinian resistance to the apartheid, racism and violence of the Israeli state. That resistance has recently been renewed on a mass scale: a popular struggle that provides a counterpoint to the Palestinian Authority's complicity in apartheid. It is complemented by a global movement of solidarity. The Palestinian cause is, in its global dimensions, a simultaneously anti-imperialist, anti-war and anti-racist cause. It brings supporters of justice for Palestine into conflict with imperialism, war and racism perpetrated by Israel's allies in the US, UK and elsewhere.

Let's begin, though, with an overview of today's apartheid reality. Amnesty International's hard-hitting report on Israel's apartheid regime, published in February 2022, was a milestone.[10] It followed reports in 2021 from B'Tselem (Israel's leading human-rights organisation) and Human Rights Watch, both of which documented the apartheid practices of the Israeli state. This third example of a major report foregrounding the concept of Israeli apartheid was especially notable, both because

of Amnesty's high profile and because of the forensic
factual detail it contained. It was also significant because
it highlighted the continuities across historic Palestine,
rather than limiting itself to the Occupied Territories of
Gaza and the West Bank.

B'Tselem's report, published in January 2021, was
centred on the notion of 'a regime of Jewish supremacy'
stretching across the whole of historic Palestine, from the
Mediterranean Sea to the Jordan River. It recognised that
apartheid varied in form in different parts of that territory,
but argued that it was best understood as a single regime
of systematic discrimination and inequality. It explicitly
countered the myth that Israel itself was fundamentally
different from the occupied territories.

The Amnesty report likewise emphasised the sweeping
and systematic character of Israeli apartheid, subjecting
Palestinians inside Israel to 'cruel policies of segregation,
dispossession and exclusion', just as Palestinians in
annexed east Jerusalem or the Occupied Territories endure
the same. These policies involve treating Palestinians as an
'inferior racial group' who are 'systematically deprived of
their rights'.

The report defined apartheid in the following terms:
'A system of apartheid is an institutionalised regime
of oppression and domination by one racial group
over another. In international criminal law, specific
unlawful acts which are committed within a system
of apartheid and with the intention of maintaining it
constitute the crime against humanity of apartheid.'

The report referred to 'a system amounting to apartheid
under international law', citing the Rome Statute and
Apartheid Convention, with a vast array of examples
of 'unlawful killing, torture, forcible transfer and the
denial of basic rights and freedoms'. It stated: 'Israel
enforces a system of oppression and domination against
the Palestinian people wherever it has control over their

rights.' This is, correctly, extended to not only Israel and the occupied Territories, but displaced refugees living elsewhere, who continue to be denied their right of return.

The report documented various aspects of Israel's apartheid system. This included the unlawful killing of Palestinian protesters, with 214 Palestinian civilians (including 46 children) killed by Israeli repression during the Gaza border-fence protests of 2018-19. This was the primary basis for Amnesty's plea to the UN Security Council to impose 'a comprehensive arms embargo on Israel'.

The report was also very strong in condemning Israel's attempts 'Judaise' many areas, showing 'that successive Israeli governments have considered Palestinians a demographic threat, and imposed measures to control and decrease their presence and access to land in Israel and the OPT'. These measures can be seen in the expansion of illegal settlements in the West Bank, the house demolitions in east Jerusalem and the brutal treatment of Bedouin Palestinian communities in the Negev region in southern Israel.

The report also criticised Israel's institutional and legal measures to condemn Palestinians to inferior racial status, especially highlighting the 2018 Nationality Law as enshrining 'systematic discrimination' against the Palestinian minority inside Israel's borders. Furthermore, it noted that Palestinians in Gaza and the West Bank 'have no citizenship and most are considered stateless.' But the most fundamental aspect of Israel's demographic control is its continuing denial of the right of return for Palestinian refugees, which contrasts with the right of Jews (wherever in the world they originate) to migrate to Israel and gain citizenship.

Amnesty's report called for Israel to be held accountable, demanding that governments stop colluding in apartheid. The report specifically calls for the International Criminal Court to investigate Israel using the apartheid framework. It said: 'There is no possible justification for a system built around the institutionalised and prolonged racist oppression of millions of people.' For this reason, it urges governments worldwide to stop trading in arms with Israel. It also warns governments that they will be on 'the wrong side of history' if they continue to tolerate Israel's apartheid system.

Crucially, Amnesty located any discussion of peace in the context of dismantling Israel's apartheid framework, saying that 'peace and security will remain a distant prospect for Israelis and Palestinians alike', so long as apartheid continues. This insistence that ending injustice is the precondition for peace and security is a long way from the familiar framing of a 'two-sided conflict' that characterised the doomed Oslo 'peace process' of the 1990s. The emphasis is on the need for Israel to end its regime of supremacy and on the international community to stop tolerating and sanctioning it.

The report constituted an endorsement of the call for state-level sanctions that the boycott, divestment and sanctions (BDS) movement has been campaigning for since 2005. The report's recommendations also echoed the aims of the BDS movement when they urged Israel to grant equal rights to Palestinians inside Israel and call for recognition of 'the right of Palestinian refugees and their descendants to return to homes where they or their families once lived', accompanied by reparations.

Amnesty's report represented a historic shift towards regarding Israel as a single apartheid regime that institutionalises injustice for all Palestinians, whether in Israel, the occupied territories or beyond. The Palestinians have a shared history and a shared political struggle for justice, freedom and equality. This ongoing struggle, which inspires widespread support internationally, is in defiance of Israel's efforts to erase Palestine: to deny that Palestinian self-determination is legitimate, to fragment and divide the Palestinian people, to erase the Palestinians from the land of Palestine.

Chapter Seven: Complicity

In May 2021, there was a wave of mass Palestinian resistance to a series of attacks, from east Jerusalem to Gaza, by the Israeli state. However, a striking element in this upsurge was the awful role played by the Palestinian Authority. It has not merely been weak and ineffectual, but has actively repressed some Palestinian demonstrations in the occupied West Bank. It represents the long-term process of incorporation into the Israeli oppression of the Palestinians documented in chapter five.

Perhaps the worst moment came with the arrest and death of Nizar Banat, a Palestinian activist, on 24 June 2021. The 44-year-old died in the custody of Palestinian security forces. Subsequent demonstrations over his death were violently attacked by security forces. No wonder an *Electronic Intifada* article in late June 2021 was headlined 'Palestinian Authority forces are Israel's foot soldiers'.

This was no aberration. It was in keeping with the PA's role in response to the uprising in May. A brief re-cap of what happened is useful here.

Threatened evictions of families in the Sheikh Jarrah neighbourhood of east Jerusalem, to make way for Jewish Israeli settlers, prompted demonstrations. The evictions were significant as part of the process of removing Palestinians from Jerusalem, but also symbolised the whole dynamic of dispossession that has characterised the Palestinian experience since at least 1948.

Israeli crackdowns on the protests prompted further street mobilisation in east Jerusalem. The storming of Al Aqsa (the third holiest site in Islam), with Israeli forces using tear gas and rubber bullets, was especially provocative and caused outrage. This generated widespread solidarity protests among Palestinian citizens of Israel and in the

West Bank.

The Israeli assault on Gaza, which killed over 200 people in just eleven days, fuelled a higher level of protest. Palestinians in Israel demonstrated on a scale rarely seen before, and were the driving force behind 18 May becoming a general-strike day. Protests took place in many cities and towns in the West Bank, partly in solidarity with Sheikh Jarrah and the Palestinians under attack in Gaza, but also fuelled by West Bank Palestinians' own deep-seated grievances.

After the ceasefire was agreed, Israeli forces went on the offensive with a wave of repression against Palestinians, especially young protesters, in Israel. This was an attempt to punish Palestinian citizens of Israel for their unusual levels of militancy, and to deter further action. In the West Bank, however, Israel has relied more on the role of Palestinian Authority forces to enforce its will.

Many Palestinians celebrated the setback for Israel in Gaza, where its military offensive was widely regarded as a strategic failure, and also celebrated a number of partial climbdowns forced upon Israel, such as a delay to the Sheikh Jarrah evictions. It was at one such public celebration in Ramallah, the seat of the Palestinian Authority, on 21 May, that Palestinian student Tariq al-Khudairi was arrested by PA security forces.

The West Bank is (following the Oslo Accords) divided into different areas, known as Area A, Area B and Area C, according to how much authority and control is delegated by the occupying power to the Palestinian Authority. Ramallah is in Area A (the highest level of relative autonomy for the PA). This means that Israeli forces intervene directly less than in many other areas of the West Bank, largely leaving it to Palestinian security forces to deal with protests. These ostensibly Palestinian forces are, in effect, incorporated into a security apparatus that oppresses Palestinians.

The PA's story about al-Khudairi was that he insulted

the late Yasser Arafat, former PLO leader, through his chanting. This should not lead to arrest, but was in any case disputed by many eyewitnesses. There was widespread speculation that the arrest, and a number of other similar arrests, was on extremely tenuous grounds, and was in fact politically motivated.

The PA, dominated by the Fatah political faction, had seen its credibility and popularity fall during the popular upsurge in May. This was against a background of already being distrusted by large numbers of Palestinians. During the wave of protests, the PA was perceived as offering no leadership to the struggle at best, and actively repressing protests at worst.

Many Palestinians in the West Bank asked why there was a higher level of struggle among Palestinians inside Israel than there was in the West Bank. The protests that did take place, and they were numerous and sometimes large, were largely grassroots affairs, with the official leadership only endorsing them under pressure, if at all. Furthermore, Fatah's main rival, Hamas, saw its popularity grow as a result of its role in Gaza.

These events prompted a new bout of discussion and debate among Palestinians about the PA's security cooperation with Israel: always a highly contentious topic, but acutely so in this context. This cooperation, which was once referred to as a case of Israel 'outsourcing the occupation' to the PA, is rooted in the Oslo 'peace process'.

The PA's crackdown in May/June 2021, symbolised by the high-profile arrest of al-Khudairi, was motivated by the goal of regaining control after the upsurge of protest and by a desire to shift the narrative, characterising activists on the ground as divisive troublemakers. There was subsequently a cycle of protests and repression, with cases of torture and physical assault by security forces documented by lawyers and human-rights groups.

The background to this is the worsening status and authority of the PA, as any realistic chance of a separate

Palestinian state has been eroded. Any credibility it once had depended upon the viability of 'peace talks', and the notion that Israel might be sincerely committed to negotiations. That has been crushed under the weight of new settlement building and the belligerence of successive Israeli governments.

Barely any of the Palestinian protesters in 2021, whether in Gaza, the West Bank, Israel, Jerusalem or across the borders in Jordan and Lebanon, looked to the PA for leadership. Nor did they regard 'cooperation' with Israel as either feasible or desirable. The PA's hope of an independent Palestinian state seems unrealistic and remote to a new generation of protesters, who have increasingly expressed demands that move beyond the 'two-states' impasse.

For two decades, most of the PA's influence has derived from the international aid it has received and its consequent role as a major employer in the West Bank: there are an estimated 80,000 personnel in the Palestinian security forces, plus tens of thousands of others who work for the PA or in closely-related networks. Yet between 2013 and 2019, there was a cut in such funding of at least 50% (mainly due to Donald Trump's disregard for it during his term as US president).

A major traditional source of moral authority has been the PLO's revolutionary history, as an embodiment of a heroic struggle for national liberation, but this has weakened the more that the PA has cooperated with the Israeli state. It also suffered a loss of authority due to yet again postponing elections to the Palestinian Legislative Council (elections last took place in 2006). The PA has more and more come to be a hollow institution limited to the West Bank, lacking moral and political authority. It is deeply complicit in the Israeli occupation of the West Bank and completely incapable of uniting Palestinians in a shared struggle with common aims.

Chapter Eight: Solidarity

Although this chapter is mainly focused on international solidarity with the Palestinian cause, it is necessary to begin by noting the international support for Israeli apartheid among major states. When solidarity movements demonstrate their support for Palestine, especially in the West, they often have to confront the complicity of their own governments, and also that of the corporate world.

There are important global forces which have assisted Israel and allowed it to get away with building illegal settlements, routinely abusing Palestinians' human rights, and inflicting collective punishment and violence on Palestinians. Israel continues to be a key pillar of US foreign policy.

The Trump administration was more militantly and belligerently pro-Israel than any other, but there remains an elite cross-party consensus in support of the apartheid state. Trump's successor Joe Biden is, like Trump's predecessor Barack Obama, dedicated to supporting Israel. This deep and constant support is influenced by pro-Israel lobbying and by the ardently pro-Israel current of evangelical Christianity among the US population, but it is primarily to do with US imperialist interests in the Middle East. This latter imperative is often underestimated by critics of Israel.

Israel has forged alliances with racist, hard-right and authoritarian regimes from Brazil to Hungary, from the Philippines to Poland. It has benefited from growing convergence with the Gulf states, led by Saudi Arabia. Israel has also developed a very wide range of economic relationships across the world, especially through utilising its expertise in everything security-related: drone warfare, surveillance technology, military hardware and much more. This has de-fanged opposition from many countries to its aggressive expansionist policies.

Israel's military occupation is expensive, especially in terms of the vast spending on a complex security apparatus. Three groups pay for its maintenance: Israeli citizens (through taxation), Palestinians (via exploitation of cheap labour), and the US (donating 'aid' which helps sustain the fragile Israeli economy). But there are also profits to be reaped. It will come as no surprise to learn there was a steep rise in the market value of the Israeli economy's military-surveillance sector in the wake of the 11 September 2001 terror attacks, for example. International oil companies, arms manufacturers, and the 'security' industry have all made handsome profits from the occupation.

More generally, the occupation and Israeli policies in recent years have proved good for business. In the words of left-wing Israeli economist Shir Hever,

'the neo-liberal policies of the Israeli government enable large companies to extract high profits with minimal regulation and taxes, and to buy government assets cheaply while the government is engaged in a rush to privatisation. Those who profit from the Israeli crisis have no incentive to help in resolving it.'[11]

Israel, therefore, 'gets away it' to a large extent because it suits the interests of political, state and corporate actors. Yet, there are also, more hopefully, some important signs of support for Israeli apartheid being eroded. These are the cracks in the wall of apartheid that help develop space for imagining alternatives to the current impasse.

Israel has historically had very strong support from American Jews (who form the majority of the world's entire Jewish population outside Israel). It has also benefited from a solid bipartisan consensus in Washington politics, with Republicans and Democrats alike reliably backing almost everything Israel does. This elite political consensus has expressed high levels of public support and sympathy for Israel. Yet in these important areas, American Jews' attitudes and US public opinion, the Israeli-US relationship is becoming very frayed.

The politics of Palestine and Israel have become more and more contested among American Jews and among Americans more generally, especially among Democratic voters. Although the pro-Israel consensus is largely holding at elite level, this decline in approval for Israel has increasingly caused concern in Israeli state and political circles. It also constitutes a challenge to Washington's foreign policy in the belly of the beast.

Over the last two decades, meanwhile, there has been a mushrooming of global popular support for justice for Palestine. In order to track this, we must return to 2000.

The Oslo process was a deeply uninspiring period for anyone looking for justice for the Palestinians. By 2000, the process was clearly exhausted. The collapse of Oslo opened up some space for re-thinking and re-framing the Palestine/Israel issue: from a two-sided conflict centred on the occupied territories to a broader anti-colonial, anti-war and anti-racist struggle.

The expansion of settlements during the 1990s made the injustice faced by Palestinians more obvious. It would become still more visible from 2003 onwards, when Israel began building its separation wall (confronting its construction would become a key focus for solidarity efforts). The eruption of the second intifada, from September 2000 onwards, encouraged the idea that resistance was possible. Israel's brutal military assault on parts of the West Bank, most famously on Jenin refugee camp, in 2002 galvanised international opposition.

A new development during the second intifada was the emergence of mass international solidarity. This was the period in which a global anti-war movement developed in response to the so-called War on Terror. Just as Israel sought to justify its violence against Palestinians through the framework of countering terrorism, aligning itself closely with the US-led military interventions, the anti-war movements worldwide made the same link from the opposite perspective.

The slogan 'Freedom for Palestine' was raised on protests against the wars in Afghanistan and Iraq, as well as major protests taking place in response to Israel's offensive against Jenin (and other targets in the West Bank) in 2002. Large pro-Palestine demonstrations took place in many European capitals and significant numbers of Muslims became active in the anti-war movement. There were also anti-war and pro-Palestine street protests in many Arab cities, providing a glimpse of what would happen with the Arab uprisings of 2011.

In 2005, as the second intifada exhausted itself, a new front opened up. As many as 170 Palestinian civil-society organisations, an astonishing array of trade unions, campaign groups, women's organisations, social centres, human-rights groups and more, launched a unified call for global boycott, divestment and sanctions (BDS) and formed the Boycott National Committee. This orientation by Palestinian activists on the global movement reflected the upsurge of pro-Palestine solidarity protests, and the global anti-war movement more widely, in the previous few years. It has also represented a shift in Palestinian organising, from the old Palestine Liberation Organisation leadership (compromised by Israel's outsourcing of elements of the occupation to the Palestinian Authority) to grassroots initiatives.

The BDS appeal has since grown into a diverse, multi-faceted and truly international movement of solidarity. It has damaged Israel's reputation and global standing, challenging governments and corporations to break their complicity in the apartheid state's routine abuses of human rights.

The international BDS movement is compatible with Palestinians' own struggles, and provides them with practical and political support. It is ongoing and sustained, rather than dependent on responding to particular events, and its wide-ranging nature (academic, cultural, economic etc) means it is inclusive and far-reaching. BDS combines making an economic and political impact on Israel with awareness-raising, as well as helping de-legitimise Israeli occupation among millions of people. It links argument and action.

South African apartheid is generally cited as the precedent for the movement. The anti-apartheid movement internationally exerted pressure on South Africa through similar campaigns, ranging from individuals participating in consumer boycotts to demands for government-level action. This pressure was combined with the collective resistance of black South Africans themselves. However futile such action may have seemed at times, in the long term it played a huge and positive role in ending a racist regime.

The logic of BDS is to challenge Israel at a systemic level: its three stated aims are 'ending the military occupation, equality for Palestinians inside Israel, the right of Palestinian refugees to their homes and properties.' The second of these is clearly compatible with those who advocate a two-state solution, since it presupposes the existence of Israel, although many would argue that Israeli society is structurally incapable of actually granting such equality. The overall effect is to broaden horizons from simply criticising particular violations: the movement's aims point to the systematic nature of the oppression of Palestinians.

These three aims also serve to unite the Palestinian people. Between them, they encompass those living under occupation in the West Bank and Gaza, Palestinians within Israel, and the vast Palestinian diaspora. This breadth directly cuts against the divisions fostered by the Oslo process in the 1990s, which promoted the idea of the occupied territories as a separate issue from Palestinians living inside Israeli borders, and from the Palestinian refugees. BDS therefore reinforces pressure for unity of the Palestinian people, supported by an international movement.

Since 2005, we have also seen periodic returns to mass mobilisation for Palestine in the wider world. There were big demonstrations in 2006 when Israel attacked Lebanon, in 2009, and again in 2014, when Gaza was under assault, and we saw huge demonstrations again in 2021. Solidarity with Palestine was often raised in the revolts across the Arab world in early 2011. The Gaza Return March of 2018 later helped push the right of return up the political agenda.

BDS promotes a narrative that can unite the Palestinians: the dispossession began in 1948, it covers the entirety of Palestine, and it is rooted in a settler-colonial project that is not limited to its impact on the occupied territories. It does not formally advocate a one-state solution, but it opens up space for discussion of alternatives that go well beyond the beleaguered vision of a separate Palestinian state.

Oslo was a defeat for the Palestinians, since it greatly strengthened division and fragmentation. The Palestinian Authority became the institutional expression of narrowing horizons and meagre aspirations. The international solidarity protests during (and since) the second intifada and the emergence of global BDS were both vital steps towards reversing the defeat.

This explains why Israel hates BDS. Successive Israeli governments have put resources into delegitimising it, desperately trying to link it with the 'new antisemitism' narrative. Israel's allies, including the US and UK, have searched for ways to prohibit, or at least obstruct, BDS campaigning. It is necessary for supporters of justice for Palestine to refute the smears levelled against the movement (as I will do in the next chapter). However, the best possible response is to build effective boycott, divestment and sanctions campaigns, expanding the space for Palestine advocacy and solidarity in the process.

Chapter Nine: Antisemitism

Historically, antisemitism has had a widely accepted meaning. It has been understood to be a form of racism. It is characterised by hatred of, or hostility towards, Jews *as* Jews. It is hostility to Jews as a group, or to individual Jews because they belong to that group.

Antisemitism was predominantly a form of racism found in Europe. It found its ultimate, and most horrific, expression in the Holocaust, which matched extreme biological racism with the mass-industrial killing capacities of modern capitalism.

In this century, though, there has been a deliberate effort to redefine antisemitism. It has been largely stripped, in this new version, of its traditional affinities with other forms of racism. Instead it has come to be reformulated as a kind of political pathology, associated above all with the left and with Muslim communities. In this version, it is often treated as part of a wider political package that also includes anti-capitalism, anti-war politics, and solidarity with Palestine. Antisemitism is conflated more and more with a highly critical attitude towards Israel.

There has been a concerted push by Israel, and by its political supporters elsewhere, to tarnish opposition to Israeli policies with the smear of antisemitism. The concept of the 'new antisemitism' developed in response to growing resistance by Palestinians in the second intifada, followed by the growth of international solidarity with Palestinians in the wake of 2005's international BDS call.

The Israeli state has become more and more strategic in its response, pouring considerable funds into propaganda and lobbying to counter this threat. An integral component of these efforts has been the re-defining of antisemitism to protect itself against criticism. This is necessary because the realities of Israel's treatment of Palestinians have only got worse.

The military assaults on Gaza in 2009, 2012 and 2014 galvanised widespread public outrage across the world, as did the murderous suppression of Palestinian protests near the Gaza/Israel boundary in 2018. Settlement building has continued, in defiance of international law and United Nations condemnation. The Nationality Law enshrined apartheid inside Israel by declaring that it is a state for its Jewish citizens only, formally sanctioning the discrimination and segregation that was already part of Israeli life.

The attacks on Jeremy Corbyn's socialist leadership of the Labour Party, between 2015 and 2019, frequently involved charges of antisemitism, or failures to deal with it effectively. The charges against the Labour leadership became progressively harsher: what began with allegations of antisemitism on the fringes, and of a party that was too tolerant of such fringes, became the routine accusation that Labour was an 'institutionally antisemitic' party.

Corbyn personally came under direct fire more and more. He would later have the parliamentary whip suspended by his successor as party leader, Keir Starmer, following the publication of a major report on alleged antisemitism in the Labour Party. Some Labour Party activists have suffered disciplinary action on spurious grounds associated, often extremely indirectly, with alleged antisemitism.

While there have indeed been instances of antisemitism from some Labour members, the evidence shows overwhelmingly that it has never been a widespread problem in the party, it was increasingly addressed in a serious way during Corbyn's leadership, and the notion that Corbyn personally was complicit was always absurd.

This is not, though, an exclusively British phenomenon. In the US there was an outpouring of vitriol directed at Ilhan Omar, a newly-elected Congress member, for critical comments on Israel that were tendentiously spun as antisemitic. In January 2019, Omar became one of the first two Muslim women to be members of the US Congress in history, alongside Palestinian-American Rashida Tlaib. Together with another new left-wing Congress member, Alexandria Ocasio-Cortez, Omar and Tlaib rapidly developed a high profile for challenging the conservative status quo in Washington politics.

In both cases - Corbyn in the UK, Omar in the US - antisemitism was being weaponised. This has proved to be a recurring theme in both countries and there have been examples elsewhere, for example in Germany and France. Antisemitism is treated as a smear tactic, cynically deployed to attack the left. This has been at its most intense when establishment forces have felt threatened by the kind of politics represented by the left.

These campaigns around antisemitism are therefore a misuse of a real form of racism, geared towards political ends: weakening, stigmatising and dividing the left. They involve ignoring or downplaying the more serious instances of antisemitism on the far right and, by weakening the Left, threaten to damage the political forces that can actually confront the growing far right and its racism. There is also a massive downplaying of other forms of racism, notably Islamophobia, which is a form of 'respectable racism' firmly in the political mainstream.

One thing that the sustained attacks on both sides of the Atlantic have in common is the question of Israel. Ilhan Omar faced a backlash due to comments she made about Aipac (the American umbrella group for pro-Israel lobbying campaigns) and its influence on US politics, and for wider criticisms of the Netanyahu government's abuses of Palestinians' human rights. The furore over alleged antisemitism in the Labour Party pivoted around how to define antisemitism. In 2018 there was a major campaign to force the party to adopt the full definition, including very controversial examples relating to Israel, proposed by the International Holocaust Remembrance Alliance (IHRA).

The IHRA code was adopted by the Labour Party's national executive committee. It treats as antisemitic such things as saying that Israel is a 'racist endeavour' or challenging Jews' right to self-determination, which in practical terms means the state of Israel. Many Jewish organisations worldwide have condemned the definition on the grounds that it extends the meaning of antisemitism to encompass fair criticism of Israel. Attitudes towards Israel have always varied within Jewish communities, which have rich traditions of anti-Zionism and of non-Zionist currents. These Jewish groups also expressed concern that it makes the struggle to defeat antisemitism harder by focusing on the wrong targets.

This does not mean that the entire weaponising of antisemitism is driven by Israel or its lobbyists. That is to grant them an exaggerated influence. Their objectives, to delegitimise opposition to Israel's apartheid regime and its violence, racism and colonisation of Palestinian land, dovetail with how significant parts of the US and UK political establishments view the strategic interests of their own countries. A great many of the attacks on Corbyn's politics were focused on foreign policy, such as his personal background of opposition to Nato and nuclear weapons, with senior figures from the British state (former generals or security-services chiefs) warning darkly about a Corbyn premiership.

The tight alliance between Israeli prime minister Netanyahu and President Trump helped open up serious cracks in support for Israel among American Jews, the majority of whom were anti-Trump. This fraying of support for Israel is part of the context for the vicious weaponising of antisemitism directed at Israel's critics in both the US and the UK. The cynical deployment of the 'new antisemitism' emerged in response to rising Palestinian resistance in the second intifada, was sustained as a response to the growth of the global BDS movement from 2005 onwards, and became more strident in response to a veteran anti-imperialist becoming leader of the Labour Party. It is now an entrenched part of the counter-offensive to support for Palestine.

Chapter Ten: Resistance

The fragmentation and divisions in the official organisations of Palestinian politics have been a recurring source of frustration for many years. The success of Hamas in Gaza's elections in 2006 came from Gazans' disillusionment with the existing Palestinian leadership, dominated by the Fatah party. The divisions between Fatah and Hamas have been a source of conflict and sometime paralysis since then. Hamas is a more complex entity than Western media and political caricatures would suggest. Nonetheless, its Islamist ideology does in some ways represent a retreat from the secular politics that once dominated Palestinian politics.

In 2021, however, we saw a remarkable upsurge of Palestinian mobilisation. There were different elements to Palestinian opposition to Israel's actions, from the armed struggle conducted by Hamas in Gaza to the street protests in east Jerusalem, from demonstrations in the cities and major towns of the West Bank, to the border demonstrations by Palestinian refugees in Jordan and Lebanon. The activities of Palestinians inside Israel were particularly notable, partly because they represented a startling break from an era of relative passivity.

The Palestinian general strike on 18 May 2021 was the first strike on such a large scale since the general strike at the start of the first intifada in 1987. It had a very strong grassroots impulse, primarily coming from below, and was political in nature. It was an expression of solidarity with families threatened with eviction in Sheikh Jarrah, Palestinian protests in Jerusalem, and the Palestinians under attack in Gaza.

It grew out of a huge number of street protests already taking place, was organised very quickly, in a matter of a few days, and was observed very widely. The dynamic appears, surprisingly perhaps, to have been that the strike call began in Israel, spread to Jerusalem, and then to the West Bank.

Fatah and Hamas both supported the strike call, but they certainly didn't initiate it. It originated inside Israel, and its spread to the West Bank was primarily through grassroots momentum. Fatah was in a highly contradictory position: while compromised by running the Palestinian Authority, it was desperate to retain a degree of popular support, especially as it felt threatened by growing support for Hamas in the West Bank (bolstered further by its relative success against Israel in the May 2021 Gaza conflict).

One of the spurs to strike action was the Israeli violence faced by Palestinians inside Israel. This was both the official violence of the Israeli state apparatus and the unofficial violence of racist, far-right gangs. The former either sanctioned or turned a blind eye to the latter. This violence was one aspect that connected Palestinians in Israel to their sisters and brothers in Gaza, Jerusalem and the West Bank, strengthening a sense of shared purpose and common identity.

The strike in Israel was a startling development because Palestinian workers in Israel do not have independent unions. They are either non-unionised or they belong to Israeli unions. It was the Higher Follow-up Committee of Arab Citizens in Israel, a nationwide extra-parliamentary organisation, that formally called the strike, though under massive pressure from below, and as part of a growing popular momentum. The strikes grew out of community self-organising by Palestinians, most obviously in response to police abuses and racist violence, not out of union activity.

Let's look briefly at one centre of struggle from where reports of the strike are available. In Haifa, Israel's third largest city after Tel Aviv and Jerusalem, the movement emerged on Sunday 9 May with a demonstration in solidarity with Sheikh Jarrah that was repressed by the police. Protests continued, however, and on Tuesday 11 May there was the first of a series of attacks by violent far-right groups (protected by the security apparatus). These galvanised further Palestinian mobilisation and community self-defence organising over the following days, out of which discussions arose about how to advance and generalise the struggle further.

The call for a general strike developed in this context, culminating in the decision by the Higher Follow-up Committee on Sunday 16 May, exactly one week after the first major solidarity protests with Sheikh Jarrah, to issue a general-strike call formally. This was complemented, significantly, by the same body publishing an appeal for global solidarity by trade unions and solidarity movements.

Monday 17 May was a frenzy of organising. Meetings were taking place everywhere. Activists visited schools to urge teachers and pupils to strike, only to find that they were already planning to do exactly that. On the day itself, Tuesday 18 May, a great many Arab shops and small businesses were closed for the day. But it went further than that: many Palestinian workers with Israeli employers courageously refused to work. Major Israeli companies were forced to make embarrassing announcements about disruption to their business or services due to the strike. Stories about Israeli employers threatening workers with the sack proliferated.

The strike action was accompanied by a great deal of community activity and collective organising to support each other. Singers and musicians gave impromptu performances for crowds, creative activities were arranged for children, and people flew Palestinian flags. The strike fed back into, and merged with, the street movement. There were protests in support of the strike, accompanied by the flying of Palestinian flags and singing of freedom songs. Confidence grew and an impromptu march was held, greeted by shouts, chants, and V signs in solidarity from motorists, with the police deciding not to interfere (almost certainly intimidated by the strength of the movement).

The strike movement spread to Jerusalem and the West Bank too. In the West Bank, there were many sizeable demonstrations on the day, with Ramallah having its biggest protest in many years. It was a very active strike, with strikers and their supporters holding street demonstrations and collectively confronting Israeli forces at checkpoints (there were a number of Palestinian deaths in consequence). The strike day – the strike itself and also the attendant demonstrations and other public activities – had a big political impact inside Israel and in annexed east Jerusalem and the occupied West Bank.

There was some direct economic effect too. Israel's construction sector relies upon Palestinian labour: around 90,000 Palestinian workers who live in Israel, plus about 65,000 Palestinians travelling daily, via the military checkpoints, from the West Bank. It is reported that on the general-strike day no more than 150 Palestinians crossed the checkpoints to work on the construction sites. A high proportion of Palestinian workers inside the borders struck too, despite threats of dismissal (and this is against the background of mass unemployment). There was clearly a sense of workers rediscovering collective economic power.

Israel, as might be expected, unleashed a wave of repression to counter the popular insurgency among Palestinians. The unusual scale of repression (unusual inside Israel's official borders, at least) was directly related to the scale, scope and social depth of the Palestinian mobilisation to which it was responding.

A *Haaretz* report by two activists in Jaffa, a small coastal city with a two-thirds Jewish and one-third Palestinian population, claimed that 'what we are witnessing now is a revolutionary spark calling for profound change'.[12] The Israeli state response must be understood, they write, as 'an institutional counter-reaction aimed at suppressing Jaffa's indigenous population.'

In Jaffa, interestingly, it was threatened evictions of local Palestinian families that fuelled the latest protest wave, a reminder that the problems faced elsewhere can also be found inside Israel. Sheikh Jarrah had powerful resonance. Starting on 10 May, Jaffa's Palestinians have endured police tactics that have been compared to a military occupation; another reason for Palestinians there to identify strongly with their sisters and brothers in the West Bank. Brutal attacks on protests have been reinforced by oppressive stop-and-search operations, routine arrests, racial profiling and the use of checkpoints.

What happened in Jaffa could be seen everywhere in Israel. The Gaza ceasefire announced on Thursday 20 May was followed by a crackdown on Palestinians who dared to continue protesting and organising. Inside Israel, there were reportedly over 250 arrests of Palestinians on Monday 24 and Tuesday 25 May. Hassan Jabareen, head of the Adalah legal centre, referred to it as 'terrorising' of Palestinian citizens by the state. This was accompanied by continuing violent attacks by groups of Jewish supremacists, generally without any repercussions from the official forces of law and order.

There had already been 1550 arrests of Palestinian protesters in the previous two weeks. Overall this has been estimated to be the largest wave of arrests and repression against Israel's Palestinian population in history. It is thought to have been even bigger than the crackdown of October 2000, responding to the start of the Second Intifada when many protests took place inside Israel. This operation was evidently designed to restore the prestige and authority of the Israeli police, which had been surprised by the scale of protests and humiliated by the strength of Palestinian mobilisation in Israel's cities and towns.

The Israeli repression was so great because the Palestinian resistance was so powerful. The lessons emerging from this remarkable wave of popular resistance will be considered in the concluding chapter.

Chapter Eleven: Prospects

There was an intensification of Israel's assault on the Palestinians in spring 2021. This included threatened evictions in Sheikh Jarrah, the storming of Al Aqsa, the brutal crackdowns on protesters in east Jerusalem, a wave of repression inside Israel and in the West Bank, and the deadly, eleven-day military assault on Gaza.

Yet this also provoked a revival of mass resistance by the Palestinians, stretching across the divides between Israel, the Occupied Territories, and the wider diaspora, stimulating a new-found spirit of unity and hope. Simultaneously, there was a resurgence of mass solidarity movements elsewhere in the world, illustrated in the UK with dozens of local protests as well as two huge London demonstrations.

The Palestinian community is divided and disparate. There are those in the occupied territories in West Bank and Gaza (cut off from each other by the siege of Gaza), and in the annexed territory of east Jerusalem. There are the second-class Palestinian citizens of Israel. There is the Palestinian diaspora in Jordan, Lebanon, Syria and elsewhere.

Political, diplomatic, and media discussion of 'Israel/ Palestine' has, for a long time, primarily focused on the occupied territories. A consensus developed, crystallising in the 1990s, that there was a 'conflict' between two sides (Israel and Palestine) that began in 1967, involving a dispute over the occupied territories, and that it could be solved by the establishment of an independent Palestinian state covering at least part of that disputed territory. According to this view, there was peaceful co-existence between Jews and Arabs inside Israel, while the refugees were frankly irrelevant, because the Palestinian right of return was not even part of the discussion.

This was always an inaccurate and inadequate picture. It ran into an impasse during the 1990s, as Israel expanded its illegal settlements while engaging in the charade of 'peace talks'. It was the instigation of the 'peace process' that ended the Palestinians' first intifada, and it was the effective collapse of those talks that laid the basis for the second intifada.

However, the Palestinian resistance of those years failed to roll back the settlement building or have any major effect on Israeli policies. This was partly because it was hobbled with an official leadership, in the form of the Fatah-dominated Palestinian Authority, that was hopelessly compromised: attached to an increasingly moribund 'two-states' vision, complicit in the Israeli occupation, and largely limited to a West Bank that was more and more estranged from the wider Palestinian community.

What does all this mean for the Palestinian struggle? The first thing to note is that Palestinians, wherever they may be, are fighting back against the injustices, violence and racism of Israeli apartheid. There has been a revival of mass struggle.

The failures of leadership in recent years are only part of the story; the flip side is the renewed popular struggle from below. There is more to the movement for Palestinian liberation than the rift between Fatah and Hamas, or the diplomatic manoeuvres of the Palestinian Authority. What is not yet clear is how this hugely impressive upsurge of mobilising and organising will affect the political landscape among the Palestinians: what level of coordination can be achieved, whether durable new organisations can be established, and whether the political dominance of Fatah and Hamas can be challenged.

The second observation is that the Palestinian struggle is happening across the entire Palestinian community, building bridges across the divides (geographical and political) that separate Palestinians, and achieving a degree of unity in action that not long ago seemed like a pipe dream. This expansiveness of solidarity is broadening political horizons too. It reinforces trends away from the bankrupt 'peace-process' model of an independent state consisting of little more than a loose network of Bantustans, towards a vision of liberation that encompasses the whole of historic Palestine.

Above all, this includes the Palestinians inside Israel. This is key. The three landmark human-rights reports in 2021 and 2022, which garnered attention partly because they referred to Israel as being guilty of apartheid, all highlighted the concerted Judaisation of the Negev and Galilee regions of Israel. Evictions, house demolitions and legal manoeuvring are used to displace Palestinians.

Even in supposedly 'mixed' communities, the reality is that Jewish Israelis and Palestinians overwhelmingly live apart. Many Jewish Israelis view Palestinians negatively, an inevitable consequence of such a divided, unequal society, and the spate of racist mob violence directed at Palestinian citizens in May 2021 should not have surprised anyone.

The protests of 2021 inspired a stronger recognition of the ties that bind all Palestinians. In Nimer Sultany's words:

'Palestinians inside Israel are protesting against Israeli policies in Sheikh Jarrah and the bombardment of the heavily populated refugee prison camp that is Gaza because they see the unity and continuity in the colonial system of oppression over all Palestinians. Our protest is asserting the unity of an anti-colonial struggle for equality and freedom.'[13]

Thirdly, the rising of the Palestinians acts as a spur to the global movement. The demonstrations in the UK in 2021 were electrified by the reality that Palestinians themselves were rising in revolt. The fact that the Gaza offensive had poor outcomes for Israel's military, and was widely perceived as a strategic failure for Israel, accentuated this.

It felt somewhat different to the summer of 2014, when

demonstrations were infused with raw anger at the terrible devastation wrought upon Gaza, but there wasn't the same inspiration that came from mass Palestinian resistance. This inspires global solidarity efforts, provides desperately needed hope, and further shifts the focus towards a broad vision for Palestinian freedom rather than forlorn pining for the chimera of 'two states'.

There was also a reawakening of active solidarity with Palestine in many Arab states: a powerful antidote to the growing 'normalisation' efforts of their leaders. This is one of the great unknown factors in the current context. It is impossible to predict whether we will see a substantial return to street protest in the wider Arab world, whether galvanised by Palestine solidarity or relating to other issues. The memory of 2011 should serve as a corrective to fatalism: it has happened before. A number of countries, notably Iraq and Lebanon, have had mass popular movements more recently.

The fresh wave of solidarity demonstrations gave new impetus to the BDS movement and began pulling in new layers to the movement, for example through student-led actions in many schools. This inevitably generates a backlash from political elites, especially through the cynical weaponising of antisemitism. In the context of British politics, there has been a concerted effort to delegitimise the cause of Palestine solidarity for some years. This requires immense ideological resources, because justice for Palestine is fully aligned with values of democracy, justice and equality, with respect for human rights and international law, and with opposition to racism.

The conflation of antisemitism with opposition to Israel does not stand up to scrutiny. Israel is a state built on the ethnic cleansing of Palestinians in 1948-49, creating a huge refugee population. It has been characterised, for the last seventy years, by dispossessing Palestinians of their land, often through force. Israel has developed a system of control that fragments the Palestinian people. Opposing all of this is a political and moral matter, not a question of antisemitism.

The resurgence of Palestine solidarity rolled back much of the slanders and abuse of recent years, re-centring Palestinian voices and experiences. The mass movement shifted the terrain of political debate, with a growing understanding (especially among younger people) that Palestine is the centrally important anti-colonial, anti-war and anti-racist cause of our times.

What's needed to sustain this, and to tilt the balance decisively away from Israel and its Western backers, is three things. Firstly, the Palestinians' own resistance must be sustained, with the connections strengthened across the divides that Israel has spent decades engineering. New generations of activists must carry the lessons of May 2021's events, including the power of collective methods like strikes and demonstrations, into the next stage of struggle, and build organisations and movements that bypass the Palestinian Authority.

Secondly, we need to strengthen the global solidarity movement. That means directing our fire at Israel but also (for people in the Arab world) at their leaders' 'normalisation' process and (for people in the West) at our own governments' direct complicity in Israeli apartheid. Palestine is a frontline of anti-imperialist politics for us. The tactics of BDS, together with further street protests, are central here. Our challenge is to build a mass anti-apartheid movement with comparable impact to the international solidarity movement supporting black South Africans during the apartheid era.

The question of what role the Arab streets can play in the next phase is a crucial one. The Arab Spring offered hope to Palestine; the counter-revolution in the Arab world, backed by the US and its allies, eroded those hopes. The relationships between Israel and several Arab states have become closer in recent years, but that can inspire strong popular opposition among the working classes of the Arab states.

Finally, we need a radically different political vision to the impoverished pleading of the Palestinian Authority leaders. The new generation of Palestinians taking to the streets is making bolder demands, insisting on meaningful unity, and broadening the horizons of the Palestinian struggle. The global movement is increasingly doing likewise.

Within the broad movement we should push for an understanding of the settler-colonial roots of Palestinian oppression, and the consequent need for an all-encompassing alternative across Palestine. Only a single, secular and democratic state can offer justice, freedom and equality for all.

References

1 Nimer Sultany, 'Peaceful coexistence in Israel hasn't been shattered – it's always been a myth', *The Guardian*, 19 May 2021.

2 Diana Buttu, 'The Myth of Coexistence in Israel', *New York Times*, 25 May 2021.

3 Ilan Pappe, *Ten Myths About Israel* (Verso, 2017), p.8.

4 Theodor Herzl quoted in Ben White, *Israeli Apartheid: A Beginner's Guide* (Pluto, 2014), p.20.

5 Chaim Weizmann quoted in ibid. p.19.

6 David Ben-Gurion quoted in Nooran Alhamdan, 'Palestinian Refugees: Myth vs Reality', *Institute for Middle East Understanding*, 22 February 2021: https://www.mei.edu/publications/palestinian-refugees-myth-vs-reality.

7 David Ben-Gurion quoted in 'What Leading Israelis Have Said About the Nakba', *Institute for Middle East Understanding*, 9 May 2007: https://imeu.org/article/what-leading-israelis-have-said-about-the-nakba.

8 Karma Nabulsi, 'Why Nakba Day Matters', *Tribune*, 15 May 2020: https://tribunemag.co.uk/2020/05/why-nakba-day-matters.

9 Pappe, *Ten Myths About Israel*, p.112.

10 Amnesty International report, *Israel's apartheid*

against Palestinians: Cruel system of domination and crime against humanity, 1st February 2022.

11 Shir Hever, *The Political Economy of Israel's Occupation: Repression Beyond Exploitation* (Pluto, 2010), p.101.

12 Yara Gharable and Hana Amoury, 'Not "Clashes" or "Riots": Here's What's Really Happening in Jaffa', *Haaretz*, 25 May 2021.

13 Nimer Sultany, 'Peaceful coexistence in Israel hasn't been shattered – it's always been a myth', *The Guardian* 19 May 2021.

Further Reading

One of the best introductory books on Palestine and Israel is *Ten Myths About Israel* (Verso 2017) by Ilan Pappé, the veteran left-wing Israeli historian who has published several other useful books on Palestinian history. Pappé's book is eloquently written and rich in historical insight but it also, as the title suggests, serves as a powerful polemical response to pro-Israel arguments. It includes a first-rate discussion of Hamas and Gaza, topics that I've largely had to ignore due to constraints of space.

Another excellent overview is Ben White's *Israeli Apartheid: A Beginner's Guide* (Pluto, 2nd edition 2014), which covers all the key bases in highly accessible style. The 'Frequently Asked Questions' section is a great source of rebuttals to defences of Israel, including the cynical deployment of antisemitism accusations. White's other two books are also well worth reading: *Palestinians in Israel: Segregation, Discrimination and Democracy* (Pluto 2012) and *Cracks in the Wall: Beyond Apartheid in Palestine/Israel* (Pluto 2018). The former is a concise introduction to apartheid inside Israel's borders, while the latter book finds hope in some recent developments, like falling support for Israel among American Jews.

Bernard Regan's *The Balfour Declaration: Empire, the Mandate and Resistance in Palestine* (Verso 2017) is invaluable on the pre-history of the Israeli state, including material on Palestinian resistance before 1948 (another topic I didn't cover for reasons of space), and it conveys the close links between British imperialism, Zionism, and the emergence of Israel. The early chapters of David Cronin's *Balfour's Shadow: A Century of British Support for Zionism and Israel* (Pluto 2017) cover similar ground extremely well, but the greatest value of the book is how it traces British complicity in Israeli apartheid (including the Labour Party's dreadful record) up to recent years.

Married to Another Man: Israel's Dilemma in Palestine (Pluto 2007) by Ghada Karmi, a British Palestinian activist and writer, is a remarkably comprehensive book that, like those by Pappé and White, is rooted in an understanding of Israel as a settler-colonial state and a commitment to a one-state alternative (its final chapter puts the case in persuasive detail).

Two books by dissident Israeli economist Shir Hever are insightful about the complex dynamics of modern-day Israel. His *The Political Economy of Israel's Occupation: Repression Beyond Exploitation* (Pluto 2010) was followed by *The Privatisation of Israeli Security* (Pluto 2018). Another book by a socialist Jewish Israeli, Jeff Halper's *War Against the People: Israel, the Palestinians and Global Pacification* (Pluto 2015), also addresses the economic basis for the Israeli state and its oppression of the Palestinians, but with a wealth of material on Israel's relationship to the wider world. It is a helpful resource for examining Israel's connections with governments and businesses globally, looking at how Israel profits from exporting its 'technologies of control'.

Timeline

1897 The First Zionist Congress in Basel, Switzerland, establishes the Zionist Organisation (later World Zionist Organisation).

1901 The Jewish National Fund is established, with a mission to acquire land in Palestine for Zionist settlers.

1916 The Sykes-Picot agreement, a secret treaty between imperialist allies Britain and France, lays the basis for the partition of the Ottoman Empire after World War One.

1917 The Balfour Declaration represents a pledge by the British government to support the creation of a Jewish homeland.

1920-47 Palestine is governed under the British Mandate, approved by the League of Nations (established after the end of World War One).

1936-39 The Arab revolt, including large-scale strike action, expresses Palestinian grievances at encroaching colonisation.

1939-45 World War Two and the Holocaust, in which an estimated six million Jews are murdered by Nazi Germany.

1947 The newly-formed United Nations formulates a Partition Plan for Palestine to replace British Mandate rule.

1948 The Nakba (catastrophe in Arabic), the ethnic cleansing of Palestine, involves Zionist terror gangs driving at least 700,000 Palestinians out of their homes, and establishes a new Israeli state covering 78% of historic Palestine.

1949 UN Resolution 194 supports the right of return for Palestinian refugees, while Israel institutes military rule on Palestinians inside Israel (which lasts until 1966).

1956 The Suez crisis sees Israel ally with Britain and

France in a clash with Egypt.

1964 The launch of the Palestine Liberation Organisation (PLO), dominated by the Fatah party, which had been founded in 1959 by Yasser Arafat and others, committed to Palestinian national liberation.

1967 Swift Israeli victory over a number of neighbouring Arab states in the Six-Day War leads to Israel occupying Gaza, the West Bank, east Jerusalem, the Sinai and the Golan Heights.

1973 Israel defeats Egypt in the October War.

1976 Palestinians in Israel take part in major Land Day protests, marches and strikes, responding to increasing Judaisation of the Galilee region of Israel.

1978 Israel signs the Camp David Accords with Egypt (leading to a peace treaty in 1979).

1982 Israel invades southern Lebanon, seeking to destroy the Palestine Liberation Organisation, and begins its occupation of territory in Lebanon.

1987 The first intifada begins, a wave of popular Palestinian resistance that lasts until 1993.

1993 Israel and the PLO sign the Oslo Declaration of Principles in Washington DC.

1994 The Palestinian Authority is formed as part of the Oslo process, with PLO leader, Yasser Arafat arriving in the West Bank to become its first president, while Israel and Jordan sign a peace agreement in the same year.

2000 The second intifada (which marks the collapse of Oslo) begins, lasting until 2005, and Israel finally withdraws from southern Lebanon.

2002 Operation Defensive Shield sees Israel make incursions into several Palestinian cities in the West Bank, with hundreds of Palestinians killed and thousands detained by Israel.

2003 Building of the Separation Wall begins.

2005 Israel evacuates its settlements in Gaza; the Boycott, Divestment and Sanctions movement is launched in July by Palestinian civil society.

2006 Hamas wins elections for the Palestinian Legislative Council, prompting international sanctions against the Palestinian Authority and the start of Israel's siege of Gaza; Israel suffers a major setback in the Second Lebanon War.

2008/09 A three-week Israeli military assault on Gaza, launched on 27 December 2008, kills 1400 Palestinians.

2014 Israel's military assault on Gaza leads to over 2000 Palestinian deaths, with more than 10,000 wounded.

2018 The Gaza Great March of Return, starting on Land Day (30 March), involves weekly Friday protests greeted by Israeli violence.

2021 A wave of Palestinian resistance, including a general strike, responds to Israel's attempts to evict Palestinians from the Sheikh Jarrah neighbourhood, violent repression in east Jerusalem and a fresh assault on Gaza.

Acknowledgements

Thank you to Sybil Cock, Elaine Graham Leigh and Bernard Regan for reading - and commenting on - drafts of the text. Thank you to Dominic Alexander and Morgan Daniels for proof reading and editing. Thank you to Shabbir Lakha for assistance with producing the book.

Front cover image: The separation barrier which runs through Bethlehem. Credit: Garry Walsh/Wikimedia Commons; used in accordance with CC BY-SA 3.0

(https://commons.wikimedia.org/).